AMYGDALA

Geraldine Alexander is an actor, writer and director, and *Amygdala* is her first professional production of her own writing. Her acting credits on stage include *Pillars of the Community* and *Strange Interlude* at the National Theatre, *Titus Andronicus* and *A Midsummer Night's Dream* at Shakespeare's Globe, *Fall* at the Traverse Theatre, Neil Bartlett's adaptation of *The Maids*, and *State of Emergency* at the Gate. Extensive television credits include *Shetland*, *Any Human Heart*, *The Government Inspector*, *Silent Witness*, *A Dance to the Music of Time* and *Poirot*. Writing work includes a workshop of her play, *My Mother's Skin*, directed by Marianne Elliott at the National Studio, and she is co-writing a TV series in development with ITV. For RADA, she has directed *Loyal Woman*, *Present Laughter* and Thornton Wilder's *Our Town*.

Geraldine Alexander

AMYGDALA

OBERON BOOKS
LONDON

WWW.OBERONBOOKS.COM

First published in 2014 by Oberon Books Ltd
521 Caledonian Road, London N7 9RH
Tel: +44 (0) 20 7607 3637 / Fax: +44 (0) 20 7607 3629
e-mail: info@oberonbooks.com
www.oberonbooks.com

A catalogue record for this book is available from the British Library.

PB ISBN: 978-1-78319-111-6
E ISBN: 978-1-78319-610-4

Printed and bound by Marston Book Services, Didcot.

Visit www.oberonbooks.com to read more about all our books and to buy them. You will also find features, author interviews and news of any author events, and you can sign up for e-newsletters so that you're always first to hear about our new releases.

Characters

SIMON NEIL
a psychiatrist (50)

CATHERINE GASSOT
a lawyer (48)

JOSHUA JAMES
the accused (Black, age 26)

The other characters; Owen, the nurse, taxi driver, lawyer could be played by two more actors or evoked by use of sound and film.

The play takes place in the present and the past going back over the last two years.

The locations in the **present** are

The interview room of a remand centre where Joshua is being held.

A room in a private psychiatric clinic where Catherine is.

The court.

The locations remembered in the **past** are

A bus, a bar, a cafe, the old Bailey, a nightclub, Joshua's flat, a beach in Suffolk, a taxi on its way to the Albert Hall and Catherine's house.

/ Indicates when the next character starts speaking.

The characters are all on stage for the duration of the play

The play can be performed with very few props – only the ones particular to the memory are necessary. The others can be mimed.

Amygdala was first performed at The Print Room Balcony, London on 25 November 2013 with the following cast:

SIMON – Jasper Britton
CATHERINE – Hermione Gulliford
JOSHUA – Alex Lanipekun

Director – Geraldine Alexander
Designer – Francesca Reidy
Lighting Designer – Joshua Carr
Composer and Sound Designer – Simon Slater

Amygdala was produced by The Print Room with support from the Arts Council England.

PROLOGUE.

The clinic in a private Psychiatric hospital.

SIMON in a Savile Row suit, immaculately dressed.

CATHERINE, wearing a loose dress, sits staring, concentrating. In the room is a large sash window.

SIMON is treating CATHERINE and talking to the audience. He clicks his fingers and studies her. He does this twice, leaving twenty second intervals. He talks to the audience.

SIMON: Her eyes are like cats; Cat's eyes.

They are impenetrable.

Catherine's trauma, has put her into a state of amnesia. Her brain has created a cocoon of forgetfulness around the pain, like an isthmus in a balmy lagoon. There is a path if I can find it, a path I must tread gently.

SIMON stops clicking.

SIMON: Catherine what did you see?

Silence.

your house…your home?

Silence.

Or your children…perhaps?

Silence.

CATHERINE: I can smell the flowers.

SIMON: Ah…yes. They're lovely – your husband sent them.

CATHERINE: Not those – I smell jasmine.

Silence.

She sits in the room looking out of the window. SIMON leaves the clinic.

I am forensically engaged with the machinations of the brain. It is currently acting as a plaster to the wound.

Remove the plaster too soon and what's underneath could become septic and never heal. I'm an expert in timing the removal of the plaster.

Sometimes, I confess, I am bored by other peoples' suffering – but Catherine's case ignited something in me.

SIMON leaves CATHERINE stays looking out of the window.

Time *the present and the past – going back over the previous two years.*

SCENE 1. DAY 1. PRESENT. PRISON.

Interview room in remand centre of a prison –

JOSHUA (26) is sitting waiting. Brought up in Croydon, of Jamaican descent. There is a table and two chairs. The presence of a guard should be felt outside the room.

SIMON comes in. JOSHUA stands up.

SIMON: No don't get up. How do you do? Simon Neil. You can call me Simon.

JOSHUA: You know who I am.

SIMON: Yes indeed I do, Mr James.

JOSHUA: Call me Joshua.

SIMON: Thank you.

> *They shake hands. JOSHUA sits. SIMON sits and gets a note book out of his pocket.*

Have you been waiting long?

JOSHUA: Not long.

SIMON: Do you know why I'm here?

JOSHUA: You're a shrink.

SIMON: Thank you for agreeing to see me.

JOSHUA: Was there a choice?

SIMON: There is always a choice.

Beat.

JOSHUA: My lawyer says you're my only chance – you're a whizz he says. Yo goin to help Cat so she can speak for me.

SIMON: I can not predict who Catherine will speak for. I have been appointed to give a psychological profile.

JOSHUA: I don want her hurt.

Beat.

How is she?

SIMON: They are taking great care of her in the clinic.

JOSHUA: How does she look?

SIMON: Physically she appears well.

JOSHUA: How do I appear?

SIMON: Sorry?

JOSHUA: How do I appear – in your professional opinion?

SIMON: Tired, wary, but that is hardly surprising.

JOSHUA: Do I appear guilty?

Pause.

SIMON: I am not here to ascertain guilt – I am here to assist Catherine Gassot. Her husband; Henri Gassot, has brought a strong case against you. You have offered no defence.

JOSHUA: Catherine is my defence.

SIMON: I have to warn you she may never come out of her present state or not in time to give evidence, and even then her state of mind may be too precarious to be a reliable witness.

JOSHUA: I'll wait.

SIMON: Will you talk to me?

JOSHUA: I can talk but it will change nothin.

Beat.

SIMON: I would like to know you Joshua.

JOSHUA: You've read the notes – you look a thorough man.

SIMON: I have read them but they are not written by you and I want to hear your version.

JOSHUA: My brain is clogged.

SIMON: Please try – it is only through talking to me that we can unscramble the events and glean the truth.

JOSHUA: I know the truth. I don need no unscrambling. I know what's at stake.

SIMON: I can help you unclog your brain. We can sift through your memories together. Truth is not as solid as we would wish, is it?

Pause.

JOSHUA: I'll trade with you. You want to talk? You want 'conversation?'

SIMON: What do you have to trade?

JOSHUA: I have gold – I have Remembrances. Tell me about your meetings with Catherine.

SIMON: There are rules of confidentiality.

JOSHUA: Describe her to me a little. Will that break the rules?

SIMON: I cannot disclose anything about my meetings with Catherine.

JOSHUA: Then I keep my memories close.

SIMON: Joshua if you don't talk to me you will almost certainly be sentenced to a long term in prison.

JOSHUA: None of that matters to me – only Catherine matters to me.

SIMON: You would do well to face the fact that at this present moment you do not matter to her, and it is in question as to whether you have ever mattered to her.

JOSHUA: I mattered. I don't need no confidential shit. I just want a description – her hair for example.

SIMON: Her hair?

JOSHUA: Yeah – how does it fall – for example?

SIMON: Softly.

Beat.

JOSHUA: Does she smile?

SIMON: Yes some times.

JOSHUA: *(He is truly grateful.)* Thank you.

Beat.

SIMON: Tell me about yourself Joshua.

JOSHUA: I am not who I was – she changed me.

SIMON: Who were you?

JOSHUA: I was loose – no family, no children nothing.

SIMON: No family –

JOSHUA: No family anywhere.

SIMON: Did you have a girlfriend, girlfriends?

JOSHUA: *(Chuckles.)* Ahhh…well I didn't sleep around. No. But one at a time an in my own time. Yeah. You got a problem with that, fine, move on. I tell it like it is.

Beat.

She got to me though. Got me so I didn't know anymore. Got me so. I wasn't certain. You know?

SIMON: I don't think I do. Do you mean you had feelings for her?

11

JOSHUA: Man. Feelings? Yeah I had feelings. Feelings so great I tingled just to look at her. I feeled her man God yeah. You mean did I love her? Could I live wivout her eh? Well I'm alive aren't I? Alive but no feelings.

SIMON: How did you meet?

JOSHUA: *(He sifts his brain to find the beginning. His memory alights on their first encounter.)*

On a bus, yeah a bus goin' north from the city.

CATHERINE leaves the clinic and walks towards JOSHUA's memory.

The Past. The Bus. Catherine and Joshua's First Meeting.

The past and the present as JOSHUA tells SIMON about the first meeting eighteen months ago.

CATHERINE, runs towards the bus.

JOSHUA: Come on you can do it!

She just makes it.

CATHERINE: Thank you. God I'm unfit. Thank you. That's more exercise than I've had in a year!

JOSHUA: You obviously don need it.

CATHERINE: Sorry?

JOSHUA: You don need no exercise – you look fit.

CATHERINE: A mirage. Good tailoring. I must sit down before I pass out.

JOSHUA: Let me help.

CATHERINE: No thank you – I'm fine.

She sits and gets out some papers and reads through making notes.

He puts his earphones on and listens to the music. He looks at her.

She knows he is looking but she doesn't let on.

His phone rings. Unhurriedly and unself-consciously he answers it.

JOSHUA: Yeah? Babe, I'm on my way. Start wivout me.

Laughs a big laugh.

Yeah I will.

Laughs. Hangs up.

She has been staring at him, she didn't mean to, but she was and he catches her eye and smiles. She is embarrassed to be caught looking and returns to her notes but drops papers – they scatter on the floor, and they both go to pick them up. Their hands touch. They look at each other.

His earphone wires get tangled up as CATHERINE tries to gather her papers adding to the muddle. She is blushing and flustered.

JOSHUA: Whoa there. You're pullin my music!

CATHERINE: Pardon. Je m'excuse. I'm sorry. My papers.

He untangles his headphones.

JOSHUA: Sit down.

CATHERINE: Sorry, you're treading on my papers.

JOSHUA: Am I?

He stoops and hands them to her.

CATHERINE: Thank you.

She tries to put them back in order.

Merdre, what a muddle.

JOSHUA: Work?

CATHERINE: Sorry?

JOSHUA: Is it work?

CATHERINE: Yes. Quite important.

She continues to try and read and sort it all out.

He listens to his music but looks at her, taking her in.

She is aware of this. JOSHUA's phone rings again. He ignores it.

She looks at him. He smiles.

JOSHUA: Naah, not bovered.

CATHERINE: Keeping someone waiting?

JOSHUA: Well.

CATHERINE: None of my business.

JOSHUA: Bit late yeah but not so you'd sweat.

The bus has stopped and is about to move off again.

CATHERINE: Oh fuck! My stop my stop.

She jumps off the bus.

JOSHUA sees some papers on the floor – he picks them up.

*JOSHUA in the **present** talks to SIMON.*

JOSHUA: She scooted off the bus but she'd left some of her papers so I jumped out after her.

SIMON: Were you near your destination?

JOSHUA: Not exactly. This was the leafy end of town, the coffee shops and bistro zone, wiv views, you know.

Past. *He jumps off the bus. He sees CATHERINE still standing trying to get her things sorted and answer her phone. He calls to her.*

JOSHUA: *(Shouts at her.)* Hey! You dropped…

CATHERINE: *(Startled.)* What do you want?!

(Into the phone.)

No. I don't know. Some guy.

(To JOSHUA.)

Are you following me?

JOSHUA: *(Laughs.)* Fuck. Calm down. You dropped some papers. I could just put them down and jump on the next bus although now I'm getting to the late late stage. I was doin a good turn.

CATHERINE: Oh.

(Into the phone.)

It's OK yes. I'll see you later. Non c'est personne. D'accord. Au revoir.

(She puts the phone back into her bag.)

I'm sorry. Thank you. I thought I had everything

JOSHUA: You said they were important.

CATHERINE: Thank you.

Pause.

I don't usually take the bus. I just saw it was going my way so… I'm a taxi addict. I like black cabs. I could buy a car with the money I spend on cabs.

JOSHUA: Me too.

CATHERINE: Really? You take taxis.

JOSHUA: Usually, it's my usual custom and now I'm going to have to.

CATHERINE: Oh of course let me give you some…

She gets out her purse. JOSHUA puts his hand out to stop her.

JOSHUA: Don do that. Here your papers.

She goes to get them.

I'll trade you a kiss.

CATHERINE: I can print them off my computer – I can manage.

JOSHUA: Really all these notes on them yeah? Then I'll just drop them in this puddle.

CATHERINE: No! Well if you want. This is ridiculous – give them to me please or get lost.

JOSHUA: *(He gives her the papers.)* We can kiss later.

CATHERINE: Can we?

JOSHUA: Mmmm. D'you fancy a drink?

CATHERINE: Aren't you late?

JOSHUA: Yep too late now.

CATHERINE: I have to go home to my family.

JOSHUA: Kids?

CATHERINE: Two.

Pause.

She shows him her ring.

Beat.

JOSHUA: Well would you like to come for a drink wiv me? – I would like you to.

CATHERINE: Thank you but no. Sorry. I have to go. Thank you for

Gestures with her papers and laughs.

She moves away.

*JOSHUA is in the **present** with SIMON.*

JOSHUA: She left an I didn know her name even.

SIMON: How did you feel?

JOSHUA: I felt stopped. Couldn get my head back straight. I wanted that kiss.

SIMON: Unlikely though surely?

JOSHUA: There was a kiss hovering from the moment we saw each other. Biding its time, waiting.

SIMON: A Hampstead lawyer stopping to kiss a young man she'd just met on a bus?

JOSHUA: You know nuffin man.

SIMON: Teach me.

JOSHUA: She turned back

SIMON: She didn't go home?

He makes a note.

Past: *CATHERINE turns round.*

JOSHUA: She turned back

CATHERINE: Actually, yes a drink would be nice.

*JOSHUA in the **present.***

JOSHUA: We went to a bar I know. Amicable, deep sofas, good wine, lightin – smoov – you know.

SIMON: Are you at ease in bars? Comfortable

JOSHUA: *(He chuckles.)* Yeah but she wasn't.

*He walks into a bar with her in the **Past**.*

They sit.

He is sprawled at ease. She is small and tense. There is an immediate connection/attraction. They can hardly breathe

CATHERINE: Your hand is on my knee.

JOSHUA: Yeah.

CATHERINE: I am Catherine. Catherine Gassot. Can you take your hand off my knee? I find it distracting.

JOSHUA: *(He leaves his hand there.)* Distracting?

CATHERINE: Worrying.

JOSHUA: Ah so you're a worrier.

He strokes her knee.

CATHERINE: I don't know that that's true. Maybe but I am anxious. I don't know you and your hand is on my knee.

JOSHUA: Joshua James. Can my hand stay on your knee now?

CATHERINE: Um um. Yes.

JOSHUA: Catherine.

He puts his arm around her and goes to kiss her.

CATHERINE: Do you do this a lot? Not that I mind but I feel I should know. I should know what I am up to here. Prepare. I don't think I mind. Not yet anyway.

JOSHUA: I am on my own, so no harm.

CATHERINE: I don't think your 'on my own' is the same as mine but. We can put that on one side.

They kiss. They breathe.

JOSHUA: Goodness.

CATHERINE: Goodness

Kiss again.

JOSHUA: I have not done this before. I have not jumped off a bus and kissed a lady like this before.

CATHERINE leaves the memory and goes back to her chair in the clinic.

*JOSHUA in the **present** talks to SIMON.*

SIMON: What did you talk about?

JOSHUA: Dunno man, can't remember but it was not awkward you know, not stilted, just flowed, chat. London, we talked about London and getting about. Transport. Her legs.

SIMON: You discussed her legs.

JOSHUA: I felt her legs. Two babies and those pins.

SIMON: She has fine legs but not exceptional in the cat walk scheme of things.

JOSHUA: Exceptional in every way; in what they led to and in what they promised and the way the shoes just wrapped her feet so perfectly. She's French you see and they know that stuff.

SIMON: Really? She seems English. Her husband is French.

JOSHUA: Don't you dare try and presume to know Catherine better than me. You pedantic shit. Her mother was French. Her father was English. She speaks French.

SIMON: You conversed in French?

JOSHUA: Sometimes.

SIMON: You're fluent?

JOSHUA: Not fluent but I speak it

SIMON: Do you speak to your family in French

JOSHUA: I have no family.

Pause.

JOSHUA: Can you go now? I've got a cell to get to.

SIMON: I understand that this is difficult for you.

JOSHUA: Get the fuck out of here.

SIMON: I am sorry Joshua. We will take it gently. It is important that we get the facts straight. The wool will tangle if we go off by even a millimeter. Please sit.

He sits.

How did you feel sitting in the bar with Catherine?

JOSHUA: You don like me do you?

SIMON: Why would you think that?

Beat.

JOSHUA: I felt good.

SIMON: Did Catherine feel good?

JOSHUA: Yeah, she felt good.

SIMON: Thank you for talking to me. Our time is up but I will be back.

JOSHUA: Will you be seeing her?

SIMON: Yes.

JOSHUA: When?

SIMON: Soon. Why?

JOSHUA: I want to know so I can imagine.

SIMON: Imagine what Joshua?

JOSHUA: That I am you, that I am there with her watching her smile and cross her ankles.

SIMON: Maybe you should imagine something else. Look where that dream has brought you.

SIMON leaves. JOSHUA stays sitting.

SCENE 2. DAY 2. PRESENT. CLINIC.

Present *CATHERINE is crying. She stops. SIMON goes into the clinic.*

SIMON: Hello Catherine.

He passes a handkerchief from his top pocket

She takes it and wipes her eyes.

SIMON: Why are you crying?

CATHERINE: I come and then I cry.

CATHERINE is shaking.

SIMON: Sometimes it is good to cry.

CATHERINE: Do you ever cry?

SIMON: Of course. Sometimes.

CATHERINE: Sometimes.

SIMON: But not for a long time.

CATHERINE: Do I know you?

SIMON: Yes Catherine – I am here to help you. I am Simon. I have been visiting you for some time now.

CATHERINE: Some time.

SIMON: I am going to show you some cards and I'd like you to tell me how they make you feel. Just look at the images if you will. Thank you Catherine.

He shows her cards with pictures on and watches her.

He shows another card.

CATHERINE: The cat and the fiddle.

SIMON: Pub or nursery rhyme?

He shows her a card. It unsettles her.

SIMON: This one upsets you – do you know why?

CATHERINE shakes her head.

SIMON: What do you remember?

CATHERINE: I remember.

Pause.

SIMON: Can you tell me why you cry?

CATHERINE: I cry because he is not with me. He is not with me.

SIMON: Who?

He shows another card.

CATHERINE: Jack be nimble, Jack be quick, Jack jump over the candle –

She up stands up suddenly and freezes.

SIMON: Catherine? Come sit down. What do you see?

Pause.

Catherine.

He goes to put his arm around her and lead her to the chair.

CATHERINE holds him.

He unwraps her.

He gives her a pill and a drink – she takes them.

CATHERINE: Merci.

CATHERINE looks out of the window.

SIMON leaves.

SCENE 3. DAY 3. IN THE PRESENT. PRISON

The remand centre.

SIMON: It comes as a surprise. Her crying.

JOSHUA: How does she cry? A detail please.

SIMON: The tears seep. They creep down her face like water in a parched river – a sorry excuse for the torrent that raged before trees were cut down and global warming did its bit.

JOSHUA: Global warmin – Sounds comforting, like a hot water bottle.

SIMON: It's the opposite.

JOSHUA: A cold water bottle.

SIMON: Vodka.

He smiles nostalgically.

JOSHUA: The opposite of comfort is devastation, bleak, relentless and brought about by us.

SIMON: But we are building dams and changing light bulbs. We go on trying. Hoping.

JOSHUA: You come to debate ecology and the oil situation? I don't care about any of that.

SIMON: Catherine is an environmentalist.

JOSHUA: A lawyer specializin in environmental issues.

SIMON: But you don't care about environmental issues?

JOSHUA: I dont' know nufin about environmental law.

SIMON: What do you care about?

JOSHUA: Music mostly.

SIMON: You were in the bar – you kissed – then – what happened?

JOSHUA: She left.

The Past *back in the bar.*

CATHERINE: I must go now.

(Looks at her watch.)

And you, you must be so late.

JOSHUA: We could eat, go to a club, we could dance.

CATHERINE: I think not, my leap on the bus can only take me so far.

JOSHUA: The cow that jumped over the moon!

CATHERINE: I'm a cow?

JOSHUA: You're a cat, Cat. Hey diddle – the cat !

CATHERINE: And the fiddle… Goodbye. Thank you for the drink.

They both leave.

Present *SIMON is in the room with JOSHUA.*

SIMON: You have kissed many women I imagine, was this one with Catherine different?

Pause.

JOSHUA: Thank you. Yeah I have kissed many woman, but if there was another word for kiss I would use that for her. Like Rodin – I 'Rodin'd' her.

SIMON: You know Rodin? You like sculpture then?

JOSHUA: Yeah I like some sculpture.

SIMON: So you wanted to see her again?

JOSHUA: Took me about a week to get round to it but it lingered you know, her mouth, nothing came close. So I thought, I'll have to follow this up a bit, not too much, nothing arranged, but it so happened I had to go on that same bus route to see my mate. Well, I got there and looked around and had a coffee. Thought I'd give it five then on to my mate's, no huge effort, just nudging opportunity a bit, coz really there was no chance, she was not me, and so I thought just see. Coffee was too strong. An espresso. But I could see her in the cup; small and elegant, exquisite. I looked up and there she was…at the counter.

The Café. The Second Meeting

Past. *JOSHUA is sitting at a table in a Hampstead café. He has a coffee and a chocolate cake.*

CATHERINE: Joshua?

JOSHUA: Hello.

CATHERINE: Why are you here?

JOSHUA: Let me help.

CATHERINE: What are you doing here?

JOSHUA: Here, let me.

He goes to help her. Takes her coffee.

CATHERINE: Thank you.

She sits. He gives her the coffee. She sips.

JOSHUA: You look well

CATHERINE: Um. Thank you. You…

I'm spilling my coffee.

JOSHUA kisses her neck. She closes her eyes looses herself for a moment. Opens them.

CATHERINE: Someone might see.

JOSHUA: They might. Cake?

CATHERINE: Non merci.

JOSHUA: Go on it's good.

CATHERINE: I don't eat cake.

JOSHUA: Why not?

CATHERINE: I don't know.

JOSHUA: Try.

CATHERINE: I can't…

JOSHUA: Sure you can

He opens his mouth and eats a mouthful of cake.

Delicious.

CATHERINE: My mother had a set of miniature scales and she weighed all her food to find its calorific value. She watched me eat like a hawk watches a fieldmouse – the sweeter the food the beedier the eyes so… I can't eat cake.

JOSHUA: Your mother is not here. I am, an this cake needs us to eat it together, it's beggin us to lick the plate clean.

He offers her the cake. She takes it, she eats it. Savours it, swallows and grins like the cat that's got the cream.

CATHERINE: Have you had a good week, has your week been good?

JOSHUA: Yeah. Busy.

CATHERINE: You look tired.

JOSHUA: Not enough sleep. You?

CATHERINE: Yes busy. I came here to work. Away from home. The children don't let me if I'm there. They want me to play and read stories and admire pictures. They made me a…

(She laughs.)

Sorry other people's children – je m'excuse… Anyway I have to get this done. I have a mountain of work to do.

JOSHUA: Are you always working?

CATHERINE: There's a lot to do.

JOSHUA: Do you ever take time off?

CATHERINE: Of course I do.

JOSHUA: We could go to a place I know

CATHERINE: What place?

JOSHUA: My flat.

CATHERINE: You live near here?

JOSHUA: Not far. We could get a cab.

CATHERINE: No. I don't have time.

JOSHUA: If you had time would you?

CATHERINE: No. I need to do my work. I want to.

JOSHUA: Good.

CATHERINE: No, no I want to, work.

Why are you here?

JOSHUA: On my way some place. Stopped off you know.

CATHERINE: On your way where?

JOSHUA: Mate's. Work.

CATHERINE: So you do work?

JOSHUA: Yeah yeah missy missy important papers! I work.

CATHERINE: Where?

JOSHUA: Here and there wherever.

CATHERINE: OK – there is no mystery you can eek from that question. It is just polite. If you don't want to tell me for some peculiar reason that is your business. It matters not a jot to me.

JOSHUA: *(Big big laugh.)* Not a jot. Cat you crack me up.

CATHERINE: I am glad I amuse you.

JOSHUA: Where did you learn to speak like that? Miss Prism bin washin your knickers?

CATHERINE: I don't know what you mean.

He takes her hand and smiles at her.

26

CATHERINE: How old are you?

JOSHUA: Ancient like Methusala and new like a bud.

CATHERINE: Twenty…eight?

JOSHUA: If you like.

CATHERINE: Ah…ah

(Smiles and sips.)

JOSHUA: You?

CATHERINE: Older. What time did you go to bed last night?

JOSHUA: Eight-ish

CATHERINE: Really?

JOSHUA: Eight this morning. I was at a party.

CATHERINE: Christ. I was dropping my children off at school
before grabbing a cab to work. You can't imagine.

JOSHUA: Neither can you.

CATHERINE: I can actually. Well I can remember coming
home from a party at eight, mascara smudging my face
and pale as a slice of English bread.

JOSHUA: Taxi tube bus?

He touches her.

CATHERINE: Metro. No need in Paris for a taxi. By thirty I was
locked in marriage and work. Midnight became exciting.
In my teens, twenties when I was studying.

JOSHUA: Come to my flat?

CATHERINE: I can't do that.

JOSHUA: Your husband?

CATHERINE: Henri is in Paris – he is nearly always in Paris.

JOSHUA: So.

CATHERINE: A walk maybe? I'd like to walk with you in the air away from here. A walk?

JOSHUA: Yeah, why not, sure, a walk. It's what people do, not me, but, yeah a walk.

CATHERINE: I'll drop my things off at home and you wait and then we could…go for a walk, if that is OK, if you don't mind.

JOSHUA: I don't mind.

CATHERINE: Here, you can finish my coffee.

JOSHUA: Did you like the cake ?

CATHERINE: Yes I loved the cake.

She leaves.

He stays waiting in the café.

*SIMON talks to him in the **present**.*

SIMON: Did you go for a walk?

JOSHUA: I waited, which is not my thing, for a long time. I waited because I know how five minutes can turn into an hour, but she didn't come. I waited, even though I knew she wasn't gonna come. I waited because I couldn't move. I was stuck there feeling a fool and my mates would not have known me. This was no chick with mile high legs and a fancy way with the hair, no, Catherine was a woman with secrets. She hadn't gone in for the shiny faced surgical look – she was just there and it did something to me. I wanted her to like me.

SIMON: Is that unusual Joshua? Most people want to be liked.

JOSHUA: I never bothered. Take me or leave me you know.

SIMON: How do your relationships usually go? Was there a pattern?

JOSHUA: I don't think so. Why? All I'm saying is that Catherine was different.

SIMON: Different from other women you had been with, in what way different?

JOSHUA: I dunno. At that moment I was suffused with her.

SIMON: How long did you stay – in the café?

JOSHUA: I was stuck welded to that Hampstead coffee shop chair. I don't know what kept me there but I could not move and my life switched tracks in that café.

SIMON: Fate took over?

JOSHUA: I don want to believe in fate. What kept me waiting was what led me here.

SIMON: I wonder why she didn't come back

JOSHUA: Once I saw her again I forgot that she didn't come. It is only now that you are making me remember that I consider it.

SIMON: It perhaps wasn't as urgent for her as you. Maybe she thought better of it. You were too young perhaps – You are twenty-four, I believe.

JOSHUA: Yeah so what?

SIMON: Age may have been a consideration, an obstacle for an elegant, sophisticated, married, middle-aged woman don't you think? It is reasonable.

JOSHUA gets up, SIMON looks towards the door. JOSHUA sits.

SIMON: Do you consider that?

JOSHUA: She had responsibilities.

SIMON: She had a choice. She could have gone back and left the children but she chose the children. She put the children first.

JOSHUA: She had responsibilities.

SIMON: She could have phoned you?

JOSHUA: She didn't have my number.

SIMON: No? – Is it possible she just forgot – that the event was not important to her.

JOSHUA: It was important.

Pause.

SIMON: Do you wish that you had never met her?

JOSHUA: That is a stupid question.

SIMON: You think so – it would be natural to wish your life back to happier times, times that didn't lead to a prison cell.

JOSHUA: Go – I can't breathe with you here.

SIMON: Time is up any way. Joshua I would like to help you.

JOSHUA: Yeah?

SIMON: Maybe there is something I can bring you? A book you want, a picture, I don't know anything to alleviate your time here.

JOSHUA: My saxophone

SIMON: I will see what I can do.

SIMON leaves. JOSHUA stays in the cell.

SIMON goes into the room with CATHERINE.

SCENE 4. DAY 4. PRESENT. CLINIC.

In the clinic. CATHERINE is standing – looking out of the window.

CATHERINE: *(She is singing a lullaby.)* Chut ma cherie,chut mon enfant fermez vos yeux ensommeilles etc…

SIMON comes in.

SIMON: Hello am I interrupting?

Carries on gently singing.

SIMON: Who are you singing to?

She stops.

Pause.

SIMON: I have been talking to Joshua. Do you know Joshua?

Pause.

SIMON: Do you remember Joshua? He knows you.

Pause.

CATHERINE: Who am I?

SIMON: You are a woman who is grieving and a woman in shock.

She slaps him. It hurts.

SIMON: FUCKFUCKFUCK!!!

CATHERINE: No swearing in court!

SIMON: Fuck forgive me. Sorry.

CATHERINE: Strike it from the record.

SIMON: I apologize. Thank you.

She sings softly; the french lullaby.

He gives her a pill and sits her down.

Pause.

CATHERINE stops singing and stares at him.

CATHERINE: Who are you?

SIMON: I am Simon – I am a psychiatrist. I am here to help you. I am your friend, Catherine.

She turns and looks out of the window.

CATHERINE: My friend?

SIMON: Yes. I will be back tomorrow.

I will be here.

CATHERINE: When the bow breaks.

He leaves holding his smarting cheek

SCENE 5. DAY 5. PRESENT. PRISON.

The remand centre. SIMON walks in.

JOSHUA: You bin fightin Simon? You look battered man.

SIMON: A slight bruise, it's nothing.

JOSHUA: If you say so.

SIMON: So Catherine left the café and did not come back – how did you see her again?

JOSHUA: Give me something.

SIMON: What can I say? Nothing has changed.

JOSHUA: What was she wearing?

SIMON: A dress.

JOSHUA: A dress – ah.

SIMON: She was wearing a dress that was soft to the touch.

JOSHUA: You touched her?

SIMON: No I no I…no.

JOSHUA: Why did you touch her?

SIMON: I helped her sit.

JOSHUA: Why did she need help?

SIMON: She didn't, I was being polite.

JOSHUA: A gentleman.

SIMON: Exactly.

So you saw her again – where?

JOSHUA: Outside the Old Bailey.

SIMON: You were waiting for her?

JOSHUA: Just passing.

SIMON: Do you often pass the Old Bailey?

JOSHUA: I hoped I might see her.

The Court. Third Meeting. Past.

Outside the Old Bailey.

He blocks her path.

JOSHUA: Hi babe. I waited.

She stares at him.

CATHERINE: I'm sorry. I… I'm meant to be in court.

JOSHUA: Can I come? Watch?

CATHERINE: Of course. It is your right.

JOSHUA: Yeah but can I watch?

CATHERINE: You'll be bored.

He puts his hand on her.

JOSHUA: I would like to watch.

CATHERINE: Comme tu veux. Court 6.

JOSHUA: Smile at me in court.

CATHERINE: I can't smile in my gown and wig. I have to be weighty and wise.

JOSHUA: Smile and I will imagine your thigh and your tongue and see if you can still be weighty and wise.

CATHERINE: Is that a challenge?

JOSHUA: No, it's foreplay

She walks into court.

*JOSHUA talks to SIMON in the **present**.*

JOSHUA: I wasn't expecting to like it –

I'd never been in court. Tried to keep out of all that and here I was.

Past. *CATHERINE summing up for the defence in court.*

CATHERINE: To find the truth we must look at the facts; make of those facts an edifice, an edifice we can enter and lie down in, stare up at the ceiling and sigh 'Ah here is the truth, we can see it and touch it. Now we know.'

My client and the corporation shared the same facts but they saw different truths. How is that possible?

My client lay down and spotted a crack in the ceiling; a crack where the truth seeped out and the rain dripped in. A crack the corporation had tried to plaster over. This crack opened to the sky and to the future; a grim future caused as a consequence of the corporation's negligence and irreverence to the truth.

She looks up and sees JOSHUA in the gallery. She smiles at him and forgets for a millisecond where she is.

Um… We, we…have different pasts; different realities and we see the world through our own lens so the facts are crucial; they are the solid boulders impregnable to opinion and experience and the truth they build stands firm.

So please, when you consider your verdict, fly over the building my client has constructed for you and see it from all angles and do not be seduced by the shiny singular story the Corporation would have you believe – it is not complete.

Farfrom jeopardizing the future my client has saved the future /of a community.

Thank you.

She sits.

Present. *SIMON with JOSHUA in the prison meeting interview room.*

JOSHUA: I was impressed – not 'out of my league impressed', but 'yeah you've got it too impressed'.

SIMON: You mean flare intellect – what did she have too?

JOSHUA: It.

SIMON: Catherine is an extremely intelligent woman – she has written books and is a leader in her field – I would agree she is impressive. What makes you think you in any way matched up to Catherine?

JOSHUA: You don know me man an I don know if I can be bothered to let you in.

SIMON: Joshua I am a professional and in spite of you I will do my job. I have a set of keys forged at university and years of practice on cases at least as complicated as this. My motives are medicinal. I want to help.

JOSHUA: Sure you do – Saint Simon of fuckin Chelsea where's your sack cloth eh? That suit tells a different story. Your motives are money and reputation. You wan Catherine weeping on your shoulder. When she cries do you take her hand? Do you stroke its silky skin with your oily digits? Do you? She is mine man an don you forget it.

SIMON: You must sit down or a guard will be forced to restrain you. You have your own cell. I expect you would like to keep it. I'm sorry if I upset you. It was not my intention. Your temper has not been your friend.

JOSHUA: Just don't…don't touch her.

He sits.

SIMON: Touching is not permitted.

JOSHUA: But you'd like to. She has this thing when she smiles, a slightly protruding tooth that means the lips are slow to replace themselves. One side is a semi quaver behind the other in realigning and in that semi-quaver I could curl up and live content.

SIMON: Your field is music isn't it?

JOSHUA: Until I met Catherine music was my life and everything else a tributary. But like I say she has it and I have it. You don't.

SIMON: Do I not? Well it seems a petty point to gloat over.

JOSHUA: It is in the detail man, the dotted crotchet that there lies any salvation any hope of sympathy.

35

SIMON: You want empathy?

JOSHUA: I want Catherine.

> **Past.** *CATHERINE comes out of the court.*
>
> *He lifts her up.*

JOSHUA: You were great. Who is going to win? You I think.

CATHERINE: Put me down. Christ. Put me down.

> Someone will see.

JOSHUA: Who will see?

CATHERINE: My husband! My colleagues – Christ.

JOSHUA: Your husband is here?

CATHERINE: Yes he is – he has a case

JOSHUA: Well he's busy then.

> *(He looks at her.)*

> OK don't sweat – you're down. There. Happy now?

CATHERINE: Thank you. I think I will win, but they are a big firm and they could come up with something I'm not prepared for. I have to be ready.

JOSHUA: Like a warrior, the best fighters are the ones that can see what's coming – it isn't force it's instinct and discipline –

CATHERINE: ...and luck.

JOSHUA: Not luck. It's never luck that I have exactly what the punters want at a gig. I can read them by the clothes, the sounds, the movement in the room. So when they come over and say Josh can you play...whatever? I say sure and they go cool and dance off happy.

CATHERINE: Can you read me?

JOSHUA: No, and that's a first.

> *He goes to kiss her she stops him.*

CATHERINE: No not here.

JOSHUA: Chill Cat. Here have a smoke.

He pulls out a joint.

CATHERINE: Christ. Do you know where we are?

JOSHUA: A court maybe?

She throws the joint on the ground and marches off.

JOSHUA: I can read her now alright: tight-arsed middle-class bitch.

Present. Remand centre.

JOSHUA: If she thought I was going to go mewling after her she was mistaken.

SIMON: You felt…humiliated?

JOSHUA: She riled me. I'd been sweet as pie, made concessions right, spent the whole afternoon in her world. I'd given a bit yeah and she wasn't prepared to even dip her fucking elegant toe into mine!

SIMON: She is a lawyer. She is married. What you were doing was illegal.

JOSHUA: Yeah. I see that now.

SIMON: Joshua why were you at the Old Bailey that day?

JOSHUA: I told you I was passing

SIMON: Yes you told me. It says in my notes that a case was brought against you for attempted rape.

JOSHUA: Yeah – an I was acquitted.

SIMON: Yes.

JOSHUA: So?

SIMON: So you had been in court? 'You had not managed to keep out of all that.'

JOSHUA: The case never made it to trial – it was thrown out because there was no case – so I never actually went into court. Don't your notes tell you that!

SIMON: *(Reading.)* It was thrown out because the accuser withdrew her charge.

JOSHUA: Because there was no fucking case.

Pause.

JOSHUA: It is irrelevant.

SIMON: Not when you are being prosecuted for rape and murder – it is not irrelevant.

JOSHUA: I was innocent – I did not rape that bitch and I did not rape Catherine – despite her husband's accusations – he knows nuffin – when was the last time he held Catherine? He's just a jealous fuckin cave man rattlin his stick!

SIMON: He's fighting pretty hard to protect her

JOSHUA: He is savin face man that's all! He can't bear that his wife, his accessory to his sterile fucking life chose a boy from the rough side. He finks I'm no one – like you do. But I am someone!!!!! I am someone! I write music, I am desired, I am wanted, I am cool, I am honest, I am lovin, I am pure, I am passion, I am flower, I am bleedin, I am cryin, I am gutted man and I love her an he is a French fuck who finks love is a silk slip and a red rose. I'm me Mr an I don lie! So fuck off to your 'weekend' with all your other enamelled fuckers and share anecdotes between sips of champagne.

SIMON: I'm not really a champagne man…

JOSHUA: Whisky?

SIMON: I don't drink

JOSHUA goes to hit him.

SIMON: I can call the guard.

JOSHUA sits.

JOSHUA: Do you smoke?

SIMON: No. Well not now, not for a while.

JOSHUA: Nor me, not now, not in here, but what I'd give…

SIMON: I will arrange that you get your saxophone.

JOSHUA: I can suck on that.

SIMON: I will see to it as soon as I can. After the weekend.

JOSHUA: Is it the 'weekend'? Well have a jolly nice time.

SIMON: Try not to see me as your foe Joshua I want to help
Catherine and if you do too then we are on the same side.
I may be your only friend.

JOSHUA: Then I'm fucked. Bye.

SCENE 6. DAY 6. PRESENT. CLINIC AND PRISON.

Present. In the clinic. CATHERINE is singing.

CATHERINE: Sonne le matina' mon petit j'espere que t' aime
ma chanson mes cherries. Je vous aime. Je vous aime.

The door opens.

SIMON: I am sorry I'm late.

CATHERINE: You have never been late before.

SIMON: I apologize.

Present. *SIMON goes into the interview room with JOSHUA.*

SIMON: I am sorry I'm late.

JOSHUA: You have never been late before.

SIMON: I apologize.

JOSHUA: Weekend took its toll?

SIMON: It was lovely, the weather was fine.

JOSHUA: I like it. It gives me a toehold.

SIMON: I was organizing your 'instrument' – a lot of red tape.
I had to go to your flat and I got lost – not really my neck
of the woods.

JOSHUA: Don't you have people to run errands; I thought you'd be too expensive to squander time tracing the AZ.

SIMON: I was curious.

JOSHUA: You can just go into my flat? Did you learn anything as you nosed about? Did you go into the bedroom?

Present. Clinic. CATHERINE dances.

CATHERINE: Don't worry we shall tell you all.

SIMON: Catherine.

CATHERINE: Do you like to dance?

SIMON: These days I don't often get the chance.

CATHERINE: We like to /dance.

JOSHUA: We like to dance

She starts to dance and so does JOSHUA.

Present. *Interview room remand centre.*

SIMON: Was there another encounter? After the old Bailey?

JOSHUA: We met at a gig. I was up next an I saw her weaving through the punters, dancin through the dark like the sun on a choppy sea

Past. A club like Ronnie Scott's. JOSHUA is waiting to go on. CATHERINE comes in. Sees JOSHUA and walks over dodging dancing couples.

CATHERINE: Hello.

JOSHUA: Well hi. You're here.

CATHERINE: I found you.

JOSHUA: You bin lookin?

CATHERINE: Oui.

JOSHUA: That's good – I've bin hoping.

CATHERINE: I saw you were playing.

Can I watch you?

JOSHUA: It's your right.

CATHERINE: But can I watch?

JOSHUA: Yeah you can do anyfing you want girl.

> *He plays his sax.*
>
> *Then they DANCE.*
>
> *They dance out of the club and into his flat.*
>
> *They freeze at the door.*
>
> **Present.**

JOSHUA: We went to my flat.

SIMON: Catherine went with you?

JOSHUA: We danced man – danced into my flat.

> **Past.** *They are in the flat.*

CATHERINE: Where are your books?

JOSHUA: Don't read.

CATHERINE: Never?

JOSHUA: I get them when I need them. Drink?

CATHERINE: *(Looks at her watch.)* Um…no thank you.

JOSHUA: I'll make you a cocktail.

CATHERINE: Sorry I feel ridiculous. I'm going. I made a mistake.

JOSHUA: Cat?

CATHERINE: I couldn't live without books. I would die of boredom. I wouldn't be able to talk about anything. My dreams would be nightmares and my waking hours dull.

JOSHUA: You've a lot to learn.

CATHERINE: I am. Maybe I should go.

JOSHUA: If you want, but then we only have to go through this again, we will meet and I will dream of you and you will think of me so let's just go to bed. You can do all this lah di dah stuff but nothing bad will happen, Cat, nothing I promise. You are here aren't you?

He puts his arm around her and she relaxes and they begin to kiss.

Present. *SIMON in the interview room with JOSHUA.*

SIMON: And you…went to bed?

JOSHUA: Yeah.

Beat.

I have sex a lot. It is something I can't do without so I wasn't ready for this

SIMON: This? Connection? Did you feel connected with her?

JOSHUA: Fuck you! I don need your vocabulary. We made love man an it was perfect.

SIMON: Better than other times?

JOSHUA: Like a poem.

SIMON: A sonnet perhaps

Beat.

But then I blew it.

Past. *JOSHUA's flat. Post-sex.*

CATHERINE: Do you sleep with many women?

JOSHUA: Yes.

Pause.

You presumably sleep wiv your husband?

CATHERINE: Rarely.

JOSHUA: Rarely is sometimes.

CATHERINE: Yes.

JOSHUA: Well then.

CATHERINE: I think I should go.

JOSHUA: What did you expect? What did you want me to say?

CATHERINE: I don't know. Sorry. I thought I was 'cool', I find I am not.

JOSHUA: Stay.

CATHERINE: No, thank you, but no. Can you call me a cab please.

She leaves.

Present.

JOSHUA: She left. No moral shit. No talk. No accusations. She just left.

He starts to cry.

SIMON: You wanted her to stay. Couldn't you have gone to a party picked up a missed opportunity?

JOSHUA: I wanted her to stay but it was no big deal. We'd been straight an it was her choice.

SIMON: Catherine chose to leave. How did that leave you feeling?

JOSHUA: I wasn't going to change for some rich bitch with a possessive streak.

SIMON: But the memory upsets you.

JOSHUA: Yeah. I wish. I wish.

SIMON: What?

JOSHUA: I wish I had lied.

SIMON: Was it the first time a woman had left you like that?

JOSHUA: Like what?

SIMON: Well, let's consider the other women in your life – had you had the same experience with any of them?

JOSHUA: She wasn't like other women.

SIMON: At the time how did you feel?

JOSHUA: She'd ruined my night. I could have been riding a girl all night I could have been at it until lunch time and had no hassle from some twitchy lady. No complicated fucking niggles.

SIMON: You mean feelings?

JOSHUA: I mean niggles – little mental ticks keeping me from being cool. OK?

SIMON: I see. I am sorry, bear with me I am trying to understand.

Present. *With CATHERINE at the clinic. Also with JOSHUA in the prison.*

CATHERINE is stroking her skin and muttering.

CATHERINE: *(Under her breath.)* Sorry. I think I should go. Sorry. Sorry.

SIMON: Catherine?

CATHERINE: I'm not talking to you.

SIMON: Who are you talking to?

So you had a fling? Catherine?

CATHERINE continues dancing.

Catherine. Why could it not just be a fling?

She keeps dancing.

Catherine sit down.

He touches her arm.

It is OK to let it go. A fling is not a bad thing.

He goes to guide her to the chair and she grabs his wrist hard.

CATHERINE: You forget yourself.

SIMON: So do you. It is my job, painful as that may be, to remind you.

He winces as she tightens her grip and then releases him.

Present. *Interview room.*

JOSHUA: I tried to erase her. I played music so loud my neighbour started knocking and he put up with a lot so it must have been real loud to make him move.

I'd blown it and I felt bad. So –

I sent her a text! Rubbish. Cardinal rule; no text and especially not at night with a drink an a smoke inside you. Aagh!

Past.

CATHERINE receives a text and reads it.

CATHERINE: I hope it was as good for you as it was for me.

Present. Prison.

JOSHUA: I wanted to get it back. I wanted to turn back the clock.

SIMON: To when?

JOSHUA: To when we were sweet.

SIMON: What did you do then? Did she contact you?

JOSHUA: No.

SIMON: She never got back to you?

JOSHUA: She didn't. No.

SIMON: Because it wasn't 'as good for her?'

JOSHUA: It was good.

SIMON: But she carried on with her life. She rejoined the world she thrived in. You must have felt rejected, spurned.

JOSHUA: She did what I did – tried to get 'back on track' –

SIMON: I want to understand how a one night stand – a rumple in the sheets can lead to this – tragedy.

JOSHUA: Let me be man. I can't help you.

SIMON: Did Catherine – see other men – besides her husband?

*CATHERINE is in the **present** still in the clinic. The spaces merge.*

CATHERINE: Men like you – rich and accomplished polished like you. Polished.

JOSHUA: Careful, don't get his hopes up. That would be unkind.

CATHERINE: Maybe we'll allow him in. Seeing as he is so keen.

JOSHUA: A threesome?

CATHERINE: Not a threesome no – but he could watch.

Present. Prison and clinic.

JOSHUA: Do you have a life or is this it, Mr Brain fuck? This; raking over the debris of other people's lives. Catherine an me, we must be a gift for you. So you wanna know the details.

SIMON: Catherine let me help.

JOSHUA: I'll just wait whilst you wank off, jism all over your notes Mr Psychiatrist Know-it-all.

SIMON: It was a fling.

It had been flung.

JOSHUA: Except it wasn't.

CATHERINE: No, it wasn't.

JOSHUA: We met again.

SIMON: Where?

JOSHUA: On a beach

SIMON: When?

JOSHUA: In another life – the life back then.

SIMON: Back when?

JOSHUA: A year ago. Real life.

SIMON: What is this?

JOSHUA: A very/ bad dream.

CATHERINE: A very bad dream.

Past. The Beach.

12 months ago.

We are in the prison and also at the beach – a memory/a dream.

SIMON in the present observes.

SIMON: The plaster is starting to come off. It is not clear yet whether this will be a sudden rip and a scream or a slow tweaking hair by hair. I have the corner up.

In Cat's eyes I can see the memory. Read it as it surfaces, and as I watch her, my mind lingers on her sensory cells.

I am more or less what you see, there are no plasters covering un-lanced boils. Of course I have scars but they are minor, useful even in gaining credibility in my field. They could mistakenly be seen as qualifications. Badges of empathy.

My marriages, there have been two, have left me with three children who I occasionally take to lunch. My life is what it should be, there are no dark corners and plenty of bright lights but…no this is not about me, it's never about the psychiatrist.

I must consult my books and clear my brain.

I always liked the sea – I had a boat once. I'd forgotten that.

CATHERINE leaves the clinic and steps on to the pebbly beach.

CATHERINE is looking out to sea watching her children and Kasia playing in the water.

CATHERINE: *(In French.)* Adam and Eve and pinch me went down to the sea to bathe, Adam and Eve were drowned, who do you think was saved?

The children laugh and splash.

(In French.)

Jean – Jacques? Isabelle? Adam and Eve were drowned who do you think was saved?

JOSHUA has walked towards her.

JOSHUA: Pinch me.

CATHERINE spins round.

JOSHUA: Pinch me, I must be dreaming.

CATHERINE looks at him, squinting into the sun.

JOSHUA: Hello.

CATHERINE: Joshua?

She pulls her towel tighter and tries to smooth her hair. She starts to totter.

Sorry a bit dizzy…the sun.

JOSHUA: *(He goes to help her.)* You should wear a hat. You'll burn.

CATHERINE: You're not my mother.

JOSHUA: No but if I was I wouldn't let you out in the mid-day sun without a hat.

CATHERINE: My children have hats.

She is really dizzy starts to wobble.

He grabs her to stop her falling.

The children start coming towards the shore. Voice; "maman, maman Qu'est que se pass ?"

CATHERINE: C'est rien. Un ami. Vous voulez un glace?

Cries of 'Oui Oui. S'il vous plais.'

CATHERINE: Kasia buy ice creams and I will see you back in the house in ten minutes.

CATHERINE waves.

JOSHUA: Your children?

CATHERINE: Yes we are on holiday. Why are you here?

JOSHUA: *(Making her sit down with him.)* Sit Cat. You conjured me here.

CATHERINE: I certainly did not.

JOSHUA: Looking good.

CATHERINE: You can't do that. You can't just appear on a beach and kiss me. What makes you think you can do that? You gave me a shock.

JOSHUA: So you've been thinking about me?

CATHERINE: No. No. What are you doing here? It's been…

JOSHUA: Five months and two weeks. I'm working – playing in the festival.

CATHERINE: We're staying in that house with friends; the cream, big, bow-fronted house. I must get back.

JOSHUA: Impressive.

He holds her hand.

CATHERINE: I look awful, I'm all sandy and salty.

JOSHUA: Not sandy,

(Licks her hand.)

Salty yeah! This is the most uncomfortable beach I've ever been on. It's not the Caribbean.

CATHERINE: It isn't meant to be comfortable. It's English.

JOSHUA: You're shiverin. Let me warm you up.

CATHERINE: No thank you.

JOSHUA: There's a man waving at you. Shall I wave back?

CATHERINE: No. I think I should go.

JOSHUA: Is that your husband? Don't go. Please. *(Pause.)* I am sorry I sent that text. Sorry.

CATHERINE: We are having a holiday.

JOSHUA: Holiday?

CATHERINE: Yes

JOSHUA: Are you havin a good time?

CATHERINE: What do you mean?

JOSHUA: Are you happy on your holiday?

CATHERINE: Yes. I –

JOSHUA: What, Cat?

CATHERINE: I never had holidays I don't know what to do with them.

JOSHUA: I can teach you.

CATHERINE: I pretend to with the children but really I am just watching – I don't know how to…join in.

JOSHUA: We don have to join in

She smiles at him.

JOSHUA: He's waving again.

She waves back.

CATHERINE: Owen – We are staying in his house. He's a client. Henri was here but unfortunately he had to leave early.

JOSHUA: Unfortunate?

CATHERINE: The children, they see him so rarely and Jean-Jacques particularly misses him, so it's difficult.

JOSHUA: So Big Man Henri is absent?

CATHERINE: I can't believe you are here. How are you here?! I feel dizzy.

JOSHUA: I'm sorry. I just saw you.

CATHERINE: No really dizzy! You gave me a shock! I need a
  drink.

JOSHUA: We can get /a drink.

CATHERINE: Water! I think I/ might faint.

JOSHUA: Water in your bag?

  CATHERINE nods.

  He rummages in her bag.

JOSHUA: Owen's coming over. Rolling up his chinos.

  She goes to the bag too.

  OWEN approaches running and shouting.

OWEN: *(Voice off.)* Leave her alone. Put down the bag.

JOSHUA: What?

OWEN: *(Voice off.)* Please leave her alone. I shall phone the
  police.

CATHERINE: *(Calling.)* It's all right Owen – he's a friend.

OWEN: *(Voice off.)* Really? You know him.

CATHERINE: Yes.

OWEN: *(Voice off.)* Can I walk you back?

CATHERINE: No, thank you for being such a white knight. I
  shall follow you up.

  OWEN retreats.

CATHERINE: Merdre.

JOSHUA: He thought I was mugging you! Christ, you lot!

CATHERINE: He was being gallant.

JOSHUA: He was being well…never mind.

  CATHERINE laughs.

  They look at each other.

CATHERINE: I must go before they send reinforcements!

JOSHUA: Come and see me tonight.

CATHERINE: Where?

JOSHUA: In the festival. Here is a pass.

He hands her a ticket – she takes it.

CATHERINE: So you are not stalking me?

JOSHUA: Nah, I'm dreamin and longin but not stalkin. This is luck man luck or a dream

CATHERINE: You're working here?

JOSHUA: Yeah. We're performing in the festival.

CATHERINE: Are you here by yourself?

JOSHUA: Come and see.

CATHERINE: I will not play games!

JOSHUA: What about Sir Lancelot – maybe he won't let you out on your own. Owen seemed somewhat proprietorial!

CATHERINE: He's nice. He's polite. He's kind and he thinks I am the bee's knees.

JOSHUA: Buzz buzz. Well I'm not inviting him.

CATHERINE: I have a husband, two children, two degrees and migraines. I slept with you once and you send me a text attributable to one of the brainless thugs I am forced to encounter in court. So do not waste my time.

JOSHUA: You like me Cat. I know you do. Please come.

CATHERINE: I might.

He smiles and she goes.

The festival. Past.

Everything disappears except JOSHUA lying on the ground and staring up at a darkening sky spinning and turning his life around.

He is on the small stage of a festival like Latitude – he picks up his saxophone and plays.

JOSHUA: Music, the rhythm of life, a pulse that reverberates and ripples.

How does sound sound? Listen – what do you hear just now? Your neighbour breathing, a cough, a humming light somewhere above your head, a rustle of sweet wrappers, a vibration from a phone on silent. Sound is the transfer of energy in the form of waves; slow waves low sound and fast waves high sound – with variations.

The possibilities! My!

Music puts a language to that sound and my music, the music I like moves effortlessly through the waves, bouncing off the air molecules and makes sound; sweet music. Music that breathes.

My music may not be the same as yours, after all we breathe different, we hear different, the waves between us change. But is there good and bad music? Are we allowed in these 'tolerant PC step careful days', is there something we can call good and something we can call bad?

Yes yes yes because some music is BAD BAD BAD.

A lie travels through the air in the same way truth does; it bounces off the air molecules and where there are no air molecules there is no sound. Outer space is silent.

Pause – he listens. Stars appear above and below him and he sees CATHERINE watching him – silence.

Silent.

Does that mean there are no lies in space? Ah... Heaven!

When I say music you will all think of something different, a memory riding a big wave from childhood or surfing through your hippocampus from a gig you went to in your teens... Maybe a rhythm is what beaches you; a percussive swell from a kettle drum.

It's all music and our preference influenced by hereditary genes, nature, nurture, alcohol, and environment makes our choices for us but there is bad music. Music that lies that distorts and manipulates the air molecules and tries to suck us in – well don' get sucked. Stay true and on that note here is my truth for you. Believe me.

He plays.

The sound of the sea and birds. It is night. Fade to dusk.

Present. *SIMON clicks his pen.*

SIMON: There is a place in the hippocampus the size and shape of an almond called the amygdala in which is stored our emotional memory. Anything in our history that is a stimulus to our emotions resides there. Catherine's amygdala is intact, Alzheimer's robs people of reason but it does not crack this nut. The kernel of Catherine is there for the picking – I am searching for the correct tool like at Christmas when the nutcrackers have been misplaced. A hammer will shatter it.

I remember my father presenting my mother with a nut every Christmas. It was an event. He would take the shell off with as little effort as possible – a silver nutcracker was used I remember. Then he would take a penknife from his pocket open it, shave the top into a point and the bottom into a base, light it and I would be asked to present it to my mother – it was a tradition. Born of love? A token maybe. They looked at each other throughout this exchange. Looked at each other without restraint. The look excluded me. One year I was invited to pass it and it went out before she received it – that year their marriage fell apart. I felt responsible for the disintegration. Foolish – a mistress in Bloomsbury and my mother's alcoholism were the cause but I felt if I had kept that flame burning none of it would have happened. That memory is in my amygdala – the sound of the sea must have brought it back. We had a house by the sea, which we stayed at every Christmas – my parents and I. I would like to go back there, set light to a nut and present it to Catherine.

The cell room reappears and JOSHUA sits waiting for SIMON. CATHERINE retreats to her window in the clinic.

SCENE 7. DAY 7. PRESENT. PRISON.

SIMON: Is what you remember the truth – your seaside idyll? A trifle rose-tinted maybe? Romantic.

JOSHUA: It was romantic. We made love everywhere and anywhere – necessity made us inventive. Sometimes just thinking of her would stop me. A phrase of music would get an extra beat or a crotchet would become a minim as my mind played on her body

SIMON: Sex al fresco – it's been your downfall.

Beat.

SIMON: Were you a 'couple'? – sometimes it is hard for a relationship to extend beyond the holiday period.

JOSHUA: She was married.

SIMON: So Henri hadn't an inkling? She didn't want him to know?

JOSHUA: It was difficult for her

She didn't want her children to know until she was sure. She was very protective of them.

SIMON: Were you jealous ever of her children? It would be natural there must have been times when their claims had priority over yours.

SCENE 8. PRESENT. DAY 8. THE CLINIC.

SIMON: What are you looking at? Catherine?

She keeps on looking out of the window.

SIMON: Look at me.

She doesn't.

There is a life Catherine, a life after this. I would like you to know that. … Catherine…there is…hope

CATHERINE: Give me back my children.

Pause.

SIMON: Catherine, shall we talk about your children about Isabelle and Jean-Jacques?

CATHERINE says nothing. She goes up to the window.

SCENE 9. DAY 9. PRESENT. THE PRISON.

JOSHUA: Catherine, how is she?

SIMON: She is…fragile.

JOSHUA: Fragile? Fragile like glass?

SIMON: Like fine glass yes. She has…retreated.

Beat.

So absolutely no one knew about your 'relationship' with Catherine.

JOSHUA: She didn't want it public, I was cool with that. It suited me.

SIMON: It meant you could still keep your options open – convenient perhaps.

JOSHUA: Yeah – but I didn't.

SIMON: You didn't?

JOSHUA: I didn't 'keep my options open'.

SIMON: But you are the man who –

(Looks at his notes.)

'Don believe in marriage' who was 'loose an happy'. It took ten months to become Romeo?

JOSHUA: Like I said, she changed me – an I changed her.

SIMON: Has it worried you that Catherine did not include you, did not confide in her friends?

JOSHUA: We kept it quiet.

SIMON: It would serve you better if it had not been quite so quiet.

Pause.

JOSHUA: I was waitin man, waitin for her to get brave. She took longer to change than me.

SIMON: She had more to lose maybe?

JOSHUA: We took off our shells y'know.

SIMON: You mean you were not who you seemed?

JOSHUA: Are you what you seem – what happens when you take off your shiny shoes? Eh? What happens when you sing true?

SIMON: I am not the issue here – I am not about to face a trial. I am not here for you to get to know me.

JOSHUA: Well I bin watchin you man, an you're in trouble.

Her eyes?

SIMON: Her eyes?

JOSHUA: Yes, how are her eyes?

SIMON: Um…her eyes…

JOSHUA: Look at me.

SIMON: *(He does.)* Her eyes are…dark and deep.

JOSHUA: Watch you don't fall in.

(He chuckles.)

SIMON: I am a professional.

JOSHUA: Yeah, course you are man.

SIMON: Did she know about the case against you? The rape case?

JOSHUA: Yeah of course.

SIMON: How did she know? You told her?

JOSHUA: She trusted me. She knew me.

SIMON: I think she did not know Joshua, it was Henri who unearthed it.

Beat.

JOSHUA: She trusted me. It was not relevant.

SIMON: Why didn't you tell her?

JOSHUA: I did tell her and she didn't care – it did not matter.

SIMON: We shall have to hope she remembers that conversation soon won't we? Time is not on our side.

Did you never argue?

JOSHUA: Nah not really.

SIMON: There is a taxi driver who says differently.

JOSHUA: Yeah?

SIMON: He threw you out of his cab. Catherine was grateful apparently. You were on your way to the Albert Hall. Don't you remember?

JOSHUA: *(Reluctantly)* Yeah I remember.

Past. The Taxi.

Past. JOSHUA and CATHERINE are in a taxi on the way to a concert at the Albert Hall.

CATHERINE: I don't know why you're asking me, it's not my decision to make.

JOSHUA: No but what do you reckon? Should I go?

CATHERINE: It sounds like a good job

JOSHUA: It is an awesome job. But it's not here.

CATHERINE: Well take it. Christ this traffic. We'll be late.

JOSHUA: We'll make it. Do you want me to go?

CATHERINE: I am married.

JOSHUA: Leave him.

CATHERINE looks at him.

Yo lips are so tight you're goin to ping apart babe. What? Would you rather I announced it. Hey babe I'm goin to travel the world. Bye babe. Is that what you'd rather?

CATHERINE: If that's what's going to happen, then why debate a foregone conclusion.

JOSHUA: SHUT THE FUCK UP BITCH, I'm talking about goin away a long, long way away an I may never come back…what can we do?

CATHERINE: DON'T YOU SHOUT AT ME… AND DON'T YOU CALL ME BITCH YOU BASTARD! Merdre.

JOSHUA: But how do you feel about it? Does reason always win out wiv you?

CATHERINE: How I feel is not your business and I don't want to influence your decision.

JOSHUA: *(Lays his head on her heart.)* All right, I'll listen to your heart.

(He listens.)

Be boom be boom be boom; it's beatin but it's not happy girl. Your heart is under strain. The rhythm may be steady but the blood is bubblin babe. You don't want me to go. You wish I'd never asked the question. You wish I would just hush up and paddle in the cool shallows where opportunity keeps a distance.

CATHERINE: *(She strokes his head.)* Yes, but mon cheri.

JOSHUA: Shhhh. Leave him.

Here

(He kisses her neck.)

A beginning

(He unbuttons her shirt and kisses her breast.)

Of happiness

(He kisses her belly.)

Let's see how long it will last.

(He goes down and between her legs and starts to pull of her pants.)

CATHERINE: The driver!

JOSHUA: Let him watch

CATHERINE: We could get arrested.

JOSHUA: Really?

CATHERINE: Indecent behavior in a public place.

JOSHUA: We can do what we like.

CATHERINE: NO! That's just it. We can't. There are responsibilities. We can not do what we want.

JOSHUA is down on the floor removing her pants. She lets him.

JOSHUA: I have responsibilities.

CATHERINE: You don't have children.

JOSHUA: Not that I know of.

She kicks him.

CATHERINE: Fuck off. I don't want to be with you. You adolescent prick.

JOSHUA: But you'd miss me eh?

CATHERINE: I'd get over it.

JOSHUA: I don't think I would.

CATHERINE: You'd live.

JOSHUA: I would not get over it.

CATHERINE: You will want children and I can not have any more – I am too old.

JOSHUA: I don't care about that – I don care about children.

CATHERINE: You think that now, but you will change, so you see my love, I can't promise you anything and you cannot see what I can see because you are young.

They separate and they both stare out of the windows.

Present.

SIMON: Was having children an issue? Do you want children?

JOSHUA: No.

SIMON: You did not imagine a life with kids and Father Christmas?

JOSHUA: Well, yeah, but no, I don care about that stuff. I never had that stuff.

SIMON: No father Christmas?

JOSHUA: No. Never.

You don plan these things.

Beat.

Past. Taxi.

CATHERINE: Merdre, we're late.

JOSHUA: Let's not go – let's go to a bar.

CATHERINE: I have clients waiting.

JOSHUA: Fuck the clients.

CATHERINE: Grow up. This is important.

JOSHUA: So is this and so is the music. It's Bach and he deserves our full attention and I can't give it to him when we are not sweet.

CATHERINE: If it is a good opportunity then take it. I cannot let you be important to me.

JOSHUA: But we –

CATHERINE: We what? There is no we – there is nothing beyond sex, your body…and music nothing. Nothing beyond the miracle of you, the necessity of you. Nothing! So fuck off and find another fool to dance with. Go.

JOSHUA: Well if you put it like that.

CATHERINE: DON'T BE GLIB. DON'T MAKE LIGHT OF THIS!

JOSHUA: Fuck you Madam Barrister! Don't tell me what to do. Safe in your Hampstead pile, fortressed by excess intelligence, some invisible French dude and children you keep so wrapped in cotton wool I fear they'll crack if I so much as smile at them. Find yourself a nice stuffed shirt to nestle up with.

CATHERINE: Maybe I will, someone kind, who won't fuck cool arsed birds in clubs as an aperitif. Someone with manners!

JOSHUA: No NO! I need no aperitif.

He pulls her towards him she struggles. He throws her to the floor.

All I want is you.

CATHERINE: You don't know me.

JOSHUA: Yeah I do – I'm the only one who knows you.

CATHERINE: I don't know you

JOSHUA: Then you aint lookin. Look Cat Look.

He pins her down.

Present.

SIMON: The driver will not be witness for the defence.

JOSHUA: I guess not. Catherine could put him right.

SIMON: But we don't know her story.

JOSHUA: Her story is my story. Listen to me.

SIMON: I am listening. You need her words Joshua. Catherine has not even mentioned your name.

JOSHUA leaves. He goes back to the remand centre.

SCENE 10. PRESENT. DAY 10. CLINIC.

CATHERINE: Simple Simon met a pie man going to the fair.

She is on the ground and starts to pull up her skirt.

SIMON: Catherine? Come and sit down.

CATHERINE: You come here.

SIMON: Catherine I will do all I can to help you.

Suddenly she grabs his wrist, twists it and pulls him towards her.

She kisses him, his neck, his cheeks, his chest. She laughs.

SIMON: Catherine stop this, stop – I am your doctor.

CATHERINE: Doctor Foster went to Gloucester in a shower of …rain What have you done with them Doctor Gloucester? Have you drowned them? Have you?

She starts to hit him. Simon has to try and calm her.

In the clinic.

SIMON: This is not your fault.

CATHERINE: Who are you? What do you want?

SIMON: I want you to tell me what you are looking at through the window. I want you to tell me about the night you forgot your children.

CATHERINE: I didn't.

SIMON: For a time they were not your /priority?

CATHERINE: Just for a moment.

Beat.

SIMON: It was more than a moment.

CATHERINE: Come here Mr Pieman-simple Simon

She pulls him towards her. He holds her and pulls her on to the ground.

SIMON and CATHERINE's speeches overlap.

SIMON: You are lying in a park with a man-who is /the man?

CATHERINE: Let's watch the sky turn black twinkle twinkle little star. How I wonder what you are. The sky is so dark, the jasmine smells sweet/ and the grass damp.

They are on the floor.

SIMON: He dragged/ you there.

CATHERINE: Carried me, cradled/ me.

SIMON: He is strong.

CATHERINE: Very strong.

SIMON: Stronger than you.

CATHERINE: Oh yes muscles, Mr Pieman sinew and no fat/ in his pies.

SIMON: Outside, with your dressing gown half on and semen seeping from your cunt and bruising on your thighs, was that just a moment of inattention?

Where are Isabelle and Jean-Jaques? Where are/ your children?

CATHERINE: The sky is huge but all I can see is his eyes.

SIMON: Whose eyes?

CATHERINE: Your eyes Mr Pieman.

She goes to kiss him. He turns her so he is on the floor and she is on top.

Can you see the sky now?

Eh? /Monsieur

SIMON: All I can see is you Catherine – you – let me help you. You are on the grass with

CATHERINE: You.

SIMON: Not me…you are on the grass with

CATHERINE: Joshua.

SIMON: And your children are

CATHERINE: asleep. They are asleep.

(She sings.)

Twinkle twinkle little star…

SIMON: What happened – Jean-Jacques woke did he? Did he wake? Did he call out? Where were you when your son called/ out Catherine?

CATHERINE: Jean is tucked up holding his rabbit and the door is open, he is dreaming and Isabelle is up a floor asleep in her room full of everything a little girl/ thinks perfect –

SIMON: That night when your children were 'tucked up' what happened?

She is looking through the window and there is JOSHUA.

JOSHUA: *(A bit drunk. He shouts.)*

Babe come nothing bad will happen. I can't live without you Cat, Cat I'm sorry /let me in. Let me in.

JOSHUA is in his cell and CATHERINE is isolated – her and her amygdala – the memory surfaces and she fends it off.

SIMON: You left them Catherine – why did you leave them?

Catherine where are you? What can you see?

CATHERINE: *(She tries to sing but falters – in French.)* Chut ma cherie, chut…

SIMON: You are in your house…are you? Catherine you are at home? Tell me what can you see?

There is a relief in speaking as if she has been bathed in light. The memory she has been living with comes to the surface. It is not until the memory is complete that she fully experiences the trauma she has been hiding from.

CATHERINE: Yes. I'm at home working. It's late, about midnight. Children asleep – a glass of wine and Mozart playing, a light shining on to my lap top, deep in concentration. Tip tap on my lap top, a car, headlights blinding through the window. I have no curtains – except in the bathroom – shutters which I keep open. At first I'm cross. Then they flick on and off and I know it's an invitation. The lights move off and I hear the engine disappearing…

*JOSHUA from his cell he is in the **Present and the Past**.*

JOSHUA: *(Softly.)* Catherine.

CATHERINE: I lift open the window – go to turn off my light.

JOSHUA: Keep it on.

CATHERINE: I hesitate.

JOSHUA: I want to look at you.

CATHERINE: I leave the light on.

Pause.

I stand framed in the window. I'm wearing a white cotton dressing gown – nothing underneath. No knickers Cat. I call 'Josh?' It's silent – just the night – just his breath-sweet Joshua music – I could imagine his mouth ajar, his lips. He's about three meters away from me. My study has a floor to ceiling window looking out over the street, there are five steps up to the door and my window is about one metre above his head. My house is on a square; a private garden in the centre, only those who have keys are allowed in. I have a key. He comes closer to the window being careful not to trample the camellia that's beginning to come into flower and reaches up. He can just about reach the window box outside my window where I'm standing.

SIMON: You didn't ask him in?

CATHERINE: No.

Beat.

I didn't ask him in. The children were asleep upstairs. I didn't want them to know about him.

Pause.

If maybe it was just a drink he'd come for and a kiss in the kitchen…but I had no knickers on and just seeing him made me wet.

We stare at each other through the window. I am so happy. I take off my robe so he can see me and the cool air bathes my skin and I just step through the window into his arms. Although obviously it was not as smooth as that; it was a bit of a stretch and it was too chilly to be naked and I hadn't abandoned all sense – yet. I go back for my dressing gown, which snags on the window frame and I tip my wine over, bang my thigh on the corner of the table and my lap top falls to the floor. I am not as light as I look and Joshua struggles to keep my feet off the cold ground. I am Alice stepping through the looking glass and for a while I'm in Wonderland.

Pause.

Kasia is out. There is a candle burning in the bathroom near the long white muslin curtain. But I'm not thinking of that.

Joshua carries me over to the garden. We have to climb over the wall although I could have gone back for the key.

Pause, she sighs.

We climb the railings and we lie down in the middle of the grass.

We are absorbed by each other.

Beat.

The fire did not rampage but it was specific. Jean-Jacques slept close to the bathroom with his door open because he was prone to nightmares and often needed me in the night – he would call to me or chat sometimes to keep the demons at bay – he must have called that night he may have screamed but they say the smoke got to him first and he would have been unconscious when he burned to death.

Pause.

Isabelle slept on the floor above in her turret and she was safe. The outside of the house looked exactly the same apart from a smudge of black by the upstairs window.

SIMON: Catherine, look at me.

She does.

You were found in the garden bruised and bleeding.

CATHERINE: Was I?

SIMON: All the evidence pointed towards an abduction. Joshua was arrested and you were taken to the hospital.

Your son Jean-Jacques is dead. Your daughter Isobel is in Paris with her father and Joshua is in prison charged with taking you against your will and thereby causing your son's death.

CATHERINE: It was less than an hour from a glass of wine and Mozart to a dead son and the loss of my lover.

She cries as the memory finally hits her. She cries as if she wished she were dead.

SIMON: I can help you Catherine. Let me help you. My darling let me help you.

CATHERINE: It was an accident.

Pause.

SIMON: If it was an accident and you went willingly you will be seen as negligent and you will not be seen as a fit parent and may well be sentenced yourself.

So is the story you told me the truth? Don't answer immediately. Think.

CATHERINE: I come and then I cry because he is not with me and, and, my son is dead and I will never see him again. The last time I felt alive my son was dying less than a hundred metres from me.

She sobs. SIMON puts his arms around her and comforts her.

She leans on his shoulder. He kisses her head. SIMON leaves.

SCENE 11. PRESENT. DAY 11. PRISON.

Remand centre. JOSHUA is sitting.

SIMON: I have come to say good bye.

JOSHUA: Good bye?

SIMON: I am sorry but Catherine will not speak in your defence, Joshua

JOSHUA: She will not?

SIMON: She can not.

Beat.

JOSHUA: A detail?

Give me something man.

SIMON: But I have no questions left. There is nothing left to trade.

JOSHUA: Catherine loves me. ME. We were making love. It was an accident.

SIMON: Because of you her son is dead.

JOSHUA: It was an accident. I would give her the world and walk away to my cell and wait to die if I thought that would help her. But it won bring her son back.

SIMON: You want to rob her of her reputation – you want to ruin her? Are you prepared to drag her through the press, expose her to the prosecutors' questions? They are not kind, they want to win.

Beat.

She will be well cared for Joshua. I will care for her. You want to do what's best for Catherine then let her come with me, let her walk away into a new life.

JOSHUA: A detail…please.

SIMON: Her kisses are hungry and she likes it when I bite her lip.

JOSHUA: You liar! You fucking fraud.

SIMON leaves.

SCENE 12. DAY 12. PRESENT. THE TRIAL – THE COURT, THE CLINIC, PRISON.

JOSHUA prepares to go into court.

CATHERINE preparing for a journey back to her old life. SIMON is with her.

CATHERINE and JOSHUA talk to each other in their heads, they cannot see each other

JOSHUA: Hey Cat.

CATHERINE: I'm sorry. You were so unexpected.

JOSHUA: So unlike what was expected. Smile. Please Cat.

She smiles – her lip catching her tooth.

Your hair.

She tucks it behind her ear. SIMON strokes her hair.

Thank you.

JOSHUA plays his saxophone – he plays true.

SIMON enters the court.

Voices heard intercut with the voices of the children on the beach.

THE DRIVER: /I chucked him out – he was threatening her.

OWEN: Please leave her alone. I shall call the police.

LAWYER: You have past convictions, not convictions, accusations.

CHILDREN: Maman /maman?

SIMON: I am afraid Catherine Gassot will not be credible as a witness for the defence. I have been unable to help Madame Gassot emerge from her post-traumatic state. To force the memory could result in a permanent damage to her mental state. This is something I am not prepared to risk. My professional opinion is that Joshua James is delusional, that he took Catherine by /force into the park.

KASIA: *(Voice off.)* Madame? Quest qui se'passe?

JEAN-JACQUES: *(Voice off.)* Maman

JOSHUA stops playing.

SILENCE. EVERYTHING STILLS. The stars come out. Space. There are no lies in space.

CATHERINE hears the silence. She hears the truth.

SIMON comes to fetch her.

CATHERINE: I just need a moment.

I want to give my evidence.

SIMON: You are not well enough Catherine.

CATHERINE: That depends on your perspective.

SCENE 13. DAY 13. PRESENT.

CATHERINE: *(She speaks hesitantly and softly.)* The truth is I love my daughter; Isabelle, and I love my son Jean-Jacques. I also love Joshua. I went into the park that night because I wanted to. I forgot my children. I forgot the candle burning and I forgot that Kasia was out. You can take those facts and draw your own conclusions but the truth is love caused this terrible accident. Love and a candle. Believe it.

The lights slowly dim and she goes towards JOSHUA.

SCENE 14. DAY 14. PRESENT.

SIMON sits isolated in his chair. Lit by one light.

SIMON: I have always kept a safe distance between me and my subject, however there are risks in looking too long.

My work has satisfied me, it absorbed and...fulfilled me to the extent that my life beyond my work is, I can say this without rancor or pain...lifeless.

Cat's eyes, were the portals. They ignited something dormant in me that I have to confess I...am surprised by. Is it called love?

The music builds and fades.

The End.

AMYGDALA

Lullaby for Jean-Jacques by G Alexander
Music by Simon Slater

Verse 1

Chut ma chérie, chut mon enfant
Fermez vos yeux ensommeillés
Montez dessus des nuages si élevés
Rêve parmi les étoiles et voler
Et je chante ma berceuse.

(Hush my darling, hush my child
Close your sleepy eyes
Soar above the clouds so high
Dream among the stars and fly
And I will sing my lullaby.)

Verse 2

Chut ma chérie, chut mon enfant
Fermez vos yeux ensommeillés
Plongez sous la mer profonde
Rêve de dauphins pendant que tu dormis
Et je chante ma berceuse

(Hush my darling, hush my child
Close your sleepy eyes
Dive below the ocean deep
Dream of dolphins while you sleep
And I will sing my lullaby)

Verse 3

Chut ma chérie, chut mon enfant
Fermez vos yeux ensommeillés
Je tu tiendrai abri du danger
Tiens – tu doucement dans mes bras
Et je chante ma berceuse

(Hush my darling, hush my child
Close your sleepy eyes
I will keep you safe from harm
Hold you gently in my arms
And I will sing my lullaby)

Joshua's saxophone story

Lullaby piano/vocal

WWW.OBERONBOOKS.COM

Follow us on www.twitter.com/@oberonbooks
& www.facebook.com/oberonbook